11+
COMPREHENSION

Series editor Tracey Phelps,
the 11+ tutor with a

96% PASS RATE

Ages 9–10

Practice

SCHOLASTIC

Published in the UK by Scholastic, 2020

Scholastic Distribution Centre, Bosworth Avenue,
Tournament Fields, Warwick, CV34 6UQ

Scholastic Ireland, 89E Lagan Road, Dublin Industrial Estate,
Glasnevin, Dublin, D11 HP5F

www.scholastic.co.uk

2 3 4 5 6 7 8 9   3 4 5 6 7 8 9 0 1 2

A CIP catalogue record for this book is available from the British
Library.
ISBN 978-1407-19022-8

Printed by Leo Paper Products, China.

The book is made of materials from well-managed,
FSC®-certified forests and other controlled sources.

Author

Tracey Phelps

Editorial team

Vicki Yates, Sarah Davies, Julia Roberts

Design team

Dipa Mistry, Andrea Lewis and Couper Street Type Co.

Contents

About the CEM test and this book

About the CEM test

The Centre for Evaluation and Monitoring (CEM) is one of the leading providers of the tests that grammar schools use in selecting students at 11+. The CEM test assesses a student's ability in Verbal Reasoning, Non-verbal Reasoning, English and Mathematics. Students typically take the CEM test at the start of Year 6.

Students answer multiple-choice questions and record their answers on a separate answer sheet. This answer sheet is then marked via OMR (Optical Mark Recognition) scanning technology.

The content and question types may vary slightly each year. The English and Verbal Reasoning components have included synonyms, antonyms, word associations, shuffled sentences, cloze (gap-fill) passages and comprehension questions.

The Mathematics and Non-verbal Reasoning components span the Key Stage 2 Mathematics curriculum, with emphasis on worded problems. It is useful to note that the CEM test does include mathematics topics introduced at Year 6, such as ratio, proportion and probability.

The other main provider of such tests is GL Assessment. The GLA test assesses the same subjects as the CEM test and uses a multiple-choice format.

About this book

Scholastic *11+ Comprehension for the CEM test* is part of the *Pass Your 11+* series and offers authentic multiple-choice comprehension activities.

This book offers:

- Challenging comprehension questions covering fiction and non-fiction.
- Targeted practice and opportunities for children to test their understanding and develop their comprehension skills.
- Opportunities for children to sharpen skills such as inference and deduction, which are an essential part of the CEM test.
- Short answers at the end of the book.
- Extended answers online with useful explanations at **www.scholastic.co.uk/pass-your-11-plus/extras** or via the QR code opposite.

How to use this book

It is suggested that your child focuses on one passage at a time and that they allow 15–20 minutes to read the passage and answer the related questions. As your child becomes more confident, reduce the time allowed in order to practise working at speed.

Your child's scores in each section will allow you to see the strength of their comprehension skills and how much more practice they need.

Comprehension 1

The *Mona Lisa*

It is generally accepted that Leonardo da Vinci's *Mona Lisa* is one of the world's most famous artworks in existence. It was painted using oil paints on a plank of wood. Art historians think it was painted sometime between 1503 and 1519, but since da Vinci did not date the painting, we are not precisely sure. The portrait itself depicts a young woman with curly dark locks, and fairly plain clothing,
5   sitting with her arms folded. In the background, a natural landscape can be seen. And of course, there's that enigmatic smile that is known the world over.

But at a mere 20 inches by 30 inches in size, visitors to the Louvre – the museum in Paris, France, where the painting currently hangs – may find themselves a little underwhelmed. Thousands of tourists flock to the Louvre every day of the year, many with the express purpose of viewing the famous *Mona Lisa*.
10   As a result, the room in which the iconic painting hangs can become extremely crowded, and it can be difficult to obtain an unrestricted view. Many visitors will also be clutching mobile phones or cameras, hoping to pose for a quick snap, which can block the view and be distracting.

The identity of the woman in the painting is one of the *Mona Lisa*'s great mysteries. Historians have suggested several different candidates for who the woman may have been. The oldest and most common
15   theory is that the painting depicts the wife of a wealthy merchant called Francesco del Giocondo, who lived in Florence, in Italy, at the same time as Leonardo da Vinci, and commissioned him to paint a portrait of his wife, who was named Lisa. In Italian, 'Mona' was a form of address used by women, just like 'Lady' or 'Mrs' in English. This theory was first put forward as early as the 1550s by Giorgio Vasari, and as a result, the painting came to be popularly known as the '*Mona Lisa*'.

20   However, in the nearly five hundred years that have since passed, some people have begun to suspect that Vasari may have been wrong. They have noticed that the woman in the painting seems to closely resemble da Vinci himself, and so they suspect that she was actually da Vinci's mother, Caterina. A third theory, and perhaps the most improbable, is that the woman in the painting was actually da Vinci himself, and that painting himself as a woman is part of the riddle.

25   Another aspect to the enduring mystery of the *Mona Lisa* is her smile. In the modern world, we are accustomed to wearing a broad grin when being photographed, but in the 1500s it was very unusual to paint a portrait of someone smiling. This was because, in a world without cameras, completing a portrait was a lengthy affair. The sitter would be required to sit perfectly still for hours or even days at a time while the artist painted, and it was simply too difficult to keep smiling for that long. The *Mona Lisa*'s
30   faint smile is therefore highly unusual, making it all the more captivating.

Today, the *Mona Lisa* is probably the most valuable painting in the world, as well as the most famous, although it is unlikely that the French government – to whom the painting now belongs – would ever choose to sell it. In 2009, a disgruntled woman threw a mug of tea at the *Mona Lisa* in a protest against the French government. Thankfully, the painting was unharmed, hanging as it does behind a thick
35   protective layer of bulletproof glass. As a result, museum officials are very concerned about the painting being attacked or damaged. A barrier has also been erected around the painting, to prevent overzealous visitors getting too close.

Carefully read through the passage on the previous page and circle the correct answers below.

1 Why are art historians unsure of exactly when the *Mona Lisa* was painted?

A. Because the date on the back of the painting is smudged and illegible.

B. Because da Vinci did not put a date on the painting.

C. Because it was painted so long ago.

D. Because the historical records have been lost.

2 'The portrait itself depicts a young woman...' (line 4)

Which of the following is the word 'depicts' closest to in meaning?

A. Portrays

B. Deceives

C. Illuminates

D. Clarifies

3 In the second paragraph of the article, a number of reasons are given to explain why visitors hoping to see the *Mona Lisa* may feel a little underwhelmed. Which of these is not a reason mentioned in the paragraph?

A. The *Mona Lisa* is actually quite small.

B. Visitors often try to pose for pictures with the *Mona Lisa*, blocking the view.

C. The room can get very crowded, making it difficult to see the famous painting.

D. The painting is situated behind a bulletproof barrier.

4 Who first put forward the theory that the woman in the *Mona Lisa* was actually a woman called Lisa?

A. Francesco del Giocondo

B. Unknown

C. Giorgio Vasari

D. Lisa del Giocondo

/4

5 Why do some people suspect that the woman in the *Mona Lisa* was actually da Vinci's mother, Caterina?

A. Because documents have recently emerged which suggest that Caterina posed for the painting.

B. Because the woman's features seem to resemble those of da Vinci himself.

C. Because it was rumoured that da Vinci revealed the subject of the portrait on his deathbed.

D. Because Caterina confessed to her sister that she did in fact pose for her son.

---

6 Which of the following is the word 'improbable' closest to in meaning? (line 23)

A. Dubious

B. Impervious

C. Unintelligent

D. Critical

---

7 Why is the *Mona Lisa*'s faint smile highly unusual?

A. Because it was rare to smile when getting a portrait done.

B. Because usually, people would flash a broad grin when getting a portrait done.

C. Because it looks like Leonardo da Vinci.

D. Because it is unclear why the subject of the painting should be smiling at all.

---

8 What are the French museum officials who look after the *Mona Lisa* most concerned about?

A. They are worried that the painting might be stolen.

B. They are anxious that people may throw beverages over the painting.

C. They are concerned that the painting may get attacked and subsequently damaged.

D. They are worried that visitors may be disappointed on seeing the painting.

/4

9 Which one of the following statements is true?

A. The *Mona Lisa* was attacked in 2019 as a protest against the French government.

B. The *Mona Lisa* is the world's most famous painting, but definitely not the most valuable.

C. The French government urgently wants to sell the *Mona Lisa*.

D. The *Mona Lisa* currently hangs behind a layer of bulletproof glass.

---

10 Which one of the following statements is true?

A. The woman in the *Mona Lisa* painting has straight, dark hair.

B. The most likely theory is that the subject of the *Mona Lisa* is da Vinci himself.

C. The *Mona Lisa* was painted over four centuries ago.

D. The Louvre no longer allow people to photograph the *Mona Lisa*.

/2

Alfred Nobel

For over a century, the Nobel Prize has been the ultimate prize for leading scientists, authors and other notable figures. Since 1901, the prestigious prizes have been awarded annually in the fields of chemistry, literature, peace, physics and medicine, with economics added in 1969. The prize ceremony is held in Stockholm, Sweden, with the exception of the peace prize ceremony, which is held in Oslo, Norway. The

5   Nobel Prize is recognised worldwide, but the story of Alfred Nobel, the man who created the award, is less widely known.

Alfred Nobel was born in 1833 in Stockholm. His father, Immanuel Nobel, initially made a living as a builder but, in 1837, went abroad to seek his fortune, leaving his wife Andriette and his sons – Robert, Ludvig and Alfred – behind, to manage as best they could. Immanuel found success during his time

10   abroad, moving to St Petersburg, in Russia, to establish an engineering company, where his family eventually joined him. The family were wealthy enough to hire private tutors for the three sons and, in 1850, Alfred was sent to Paris to study chemical engineering. He was deeply fascinated by the field of explosives, especially by the properties of nitroglycerine. Alfred soon discovered that if he mixed the compound with silica, it lessened its explosive power; Alfred had the vision to realise that his new

15   invention, dynamite – which he patented in 1867 – had the potential to revolutionise mining practices and the building industry.

Dynamite can be very useful – when constructing tunnels, in mining and in demolishing buildings. Before dynamite was invented, many of these tasks had to be completed by hand, which was very slow and very expensive. However, the problem is that the same technology can also be used to make

20   powerful weapons. Alfred went on to open weapons factories across Europe which manufactured deadly military explosives, and he became a very wealthy man.

In 1888, Alfred was astonished to read an article in a French newspaper reporting on his own death. It was actually Alfred's brother Ludvig who had recently died, but the newspaper had mixed up the two brothers and had written Alfred's obituary in error. The article was less than complimentary; the

25   journalist branded Alfred a murderer and roundly blamed him for the deaths that his inventions had caused.

Alfred was very upset by this, and began to worry about what kind of legacy he would leave after his death. He instructed his lawyers to change his will, in which he specified that his vast wealth was to be used to reward those who have 'benefited mankind'. Alfred died in 1896 in Milan, Italy, at the age of

30   63. In 1897, the Nobel Foundation was established to commence awarding the prizes – which were originally £8000 per recipient. Today, a Nobel Prize winner receives a medal and a diploma, presented by the King of Sweden, and prize money of nearly £900,000.

Carefully read through the passage on the previous page and circle the correct answers below.

1 What does the phrase 'notable figures' mean in this context? (line 2)

A. Famous statues

B. Large numbers

C. Exceptional people

D. Well-known politicians

2 'The article was less than complimentary' (line 24)

Which of the following is the phrase 'less than complimentary' closest to in meaning?

A. Congratulatory

B. Condemnatory

C. Judiciously

D. Adulatory

3 How old was Alfred when his father went abroad to seek his fortune?

A. He was four years old.

B. He was seven years old.

C. He was 17 years old.

D. He wasn't even born.

4 Which one of the following statements is true?

A. The prize money in 1901 was less than 1% of what it is today.

B. Nobel Prize medals are presented to recipients by the King of Norway.

C. The Nobel Committee was set up by Alfred before he died, in order to look after his vast wealth.

D. Alfred Nobel died in 1897.

/4

5 Which of the following statements about dynamite is not true?

   A. It can be used when demolishing buildings.

   B. It is too dangerous to use dynamite when digging tunnels.

   C. Dynamite made some tasks both quicker and cheaper.

   D. The same technology can also be used to make weapons.

6 According to the text, which of the following statements is not true?

   A. The Nobel Prize for economics is awarded in Stockholm, Sweden.

   B. Alfred Nobel was just 34 years old when he patented his invention of dynamite.

   C. False reports of Nobel's death were announced in the French press.

   D. The first Nobel Prize for peace was awarded in 1969.

7 Which one of the following statements is true?

   A. Nobel squandered his vast wealth in his later years and died in relative poverty.

   B. Nobel Prizes are awarded every two years to people who have 'benefited mankind'.

   C. After the publication of the newspaper article in 1888, Nobel was charged with murder.

   D. Nobel was driven to amending his will after reading his own 'obituary'.

8 In which country did Nobel complete his formal education?

   A. Sweden

   B. Norway

   C. France

   D. Russia

/4

9 Which of the following locations does the text not mention Nobel visiting during his life?

A. St Petersburg

B. Oslo

C. Stockholm

D. Milan

10 What was Alfred Nobel's father's occupation when Alfred was a baby?

A. He was an engineer.

B. He made his living as a doctor.

C. He worked in the construction industry.

D. He was a chemist.

/2

Comprehension 3

Jane Austen

Jane Austen was born in Steventon, Hampshire, on 16 December 1775 and was the seventh of eight children. Her father, George Austen, was the rector at the local church. Jane had only one sister – Cassandra, born in January 1773 – to whom she was extremely close. When Cassandra was sent to further her education in Oxford, Jane insisted upon attending the same school. After a while, the fees
5 became too much of a financial burden for the reverend and Jane was forced to complete her education at home by reading books from her father's extensively stocked library. She read short stories and popular novels, and her parents actively encouraged her pronounced fascination for writing by providing Jane with a generous supply of paper, fountain pens and ink. Jane's entire family would gather in the drawing room after dinner and read and listen to her recite her many poems and stories. Jane then began
10 to write novels and, although none were published at this time, she was eventually able to see them in print several years later.

In 1796, just three days before Christmas, Jane met and fell in love with a dashing young Irish barrister by the name of Tom Lefroy. She was well aware that being a woman in Regency England meant being ruled by men and that a 'good' marriage to a rich and successful man was absolutely essential
15 for a woman's future financial security. At the time, any money or property that a woman owned would become the property of her husband upon her marriage, so the only women with any degree of independence were most likely to be wealthy widows who had been astute enough never to remarry. Sadly, for Jane, Tom Lefroy had no money of his own, so her parents forbade the union. Tom was subsequently and suddenly 'called away' and Jane was never to see him again.

20 In 1801, George Austen retired and, shortly after, the family moved to Sydney House in Bath. Jane hated it and was distraught to have had to leave the only home – the Rectory in Steventon – she had ever known; she became depressed and barely put a word down on paper for months.

A year later, Jane was introduced to the wealthy Harris Bigg-Wither who very quickly – within a fortnight – asked Jane to become his wife. She accepted his proposal but soon came to realise that
25 her fiancé was a somewhat arrogant, tedious man who possessed no charm or good manners or, indeed, interesting conversation. Jane decided that, like all the heroines in her novels, she should only marry for love and she broke off their engagement within a week of it being announced. Sadly, unlike her own fictitious heroines, Jane was destined never to experience true love. Jane's resolution not to marry Bigg-Wither was a brave decision because marriage to a wealthy man would have meant financial security for
30 her and, indeed, her whole family, who were subsequently left desperately short of money when George Austen died very suddenly and unexpectedly in 1805.

Jane Austen's first novel to be published was originally titled *Elinor and Marianne* but when her older brother, Henry, persuaded bookseller Thomas Egerton to publish the work in 1811, it had been retitled *Sense and Sensibility* and the author was simply accredited as 'A Lady'. The book sold well enough for
35 *Pride and Prejudice* to follow in 1813, again with the author's identity undisclosed. *Mansfield Park* appeared in print two years later.

Jane Austen was not an influential writer and was viewed as a minor author during her lifetime; contemporary authors such as Mary Wollstonecraft enjoyed much more success. Austen's *Persuasion* and later *Northanger Abbey*, published after her death, were the first to reveal the identity of the author, and
40 her work has been in print ever since.

Jane Austen died on 18th July 1817 in Winchester and is laid to rest in the city's cathedral.

Carefully read through the passage on the previous page and above and circle the correct answers below.

1 How many times was Jane Austen married?

A. Twice

B. Just once

C. Three times

D. Jane Austen never married.

---

2 What was the original title of Jane Austen's first book to be published?

A. *Sense and Sensibility*

B. *Pride and Prejudice*

C. *Elinor and Marianne*

D. *Mansfield Park*

---

3 Which of the following statements is true?

A. George Austen's health gradually deteriorated after his retirement.

B. The love of Jane Austen's life was originally from Ireland.

C. Jane's brother Henry was younger than her.

D. Harris Bigg-Wither was a charming man but he had no money of his own.

/3

4 How soon after their first meeting did Harris Bigg-Wither ask Jane to marry him?

A. Within a week

B. Within a year

C. Within 24 hours

D. Within two weeks

---

5 How old was Jane Austen when she died?

A. Just 41 years old

B. She was 42 years of age.

C. Just 31 years old

D. She was 43 years old.

---

6 In which year was *Mansfield Park* first published?

A. 1813

B. 1815

C. 1811

D. 1805

---

7 What was the name of Jane Austen's beloved childhood home?

A. The Vicarage

B. Sydney House

C. Bath Street

D. The Rectory

/4

8 On which of Jane Austen's novels was she first named as the author?

A. *Persuasion*

B. *Northanger Abbey*

C. *Mansfield Park*

D. *Sense and Sensibility*

---

9 Which one of the following statements is not true?

A. Jane was 21 years of age when she first met Tom Lefroy.

B. Jane initially attended a school in Bath before completing her education at home.

C. All of Jane Austen's fictional characters married for love, not wealth.

D. Thomas Egerton worked as a bookseller.

---

10 How much older than Jane was her sister Cassandra?

A. Two years and 10 months

B. Three years and 11 months

C. Two years and 11 months

D. Three years and nine months

/3

Comprehension 4

San Francisco

San Francisco is situated in the western American state of California. The city has 43 hills, most of which are incredibly steep, so cable trams are a popular mode of transport for locals and tourists alike. The iconic vehicles have been serving the city for over 150 years, when they replaced the traditional horse-drawn cabs that would often struggle to cope with San Francisco's challenging gradients.

5 The city was a sleepy fishing village until, in January 1848, a local carpenter named James Marshall made a discovery that was to transform the region – gold. During the ensuing, frantic Gold Rush that occurred, astute observers realised that accessibility to the region was key. San Francisco was separated from the northerly Marin Headlands by a narrow 120-metre-deep body of water known as the Golden Gate Strait. Ambitious engineers eagerly submitted their designs for a bridge-building project

10 to the city's authorities that same year. At the time, the only route across the Golden Gate Strait was via a slow, irregular ferry service. Various proposals were submitted and rejected over the next few decades, and it wasn't until 1916 that a viable option was mooted by a former engineering student named James Wilkins.

Wilkins' proposals were costed at an astonishing $100 million, so the city's official engineer, Michael

15 O'Shaughnessy, began talks with other engineers to see if the costs could be reduced.

Poet and engineer Joseph Strauss – from Chicago – submitted a fully costed alternative proposal and won the contract. But by this time – 1929 – the Great Depression had begun to bite, and the economy had shrunk, so it was to be almost four years before building works finally commenced.

The construction of the Golden Gate Bridge proved challenging due to extreme weather conditions,

20 in addition to the perilous cliffs surrounding it. The bridge consists of two towers that stand 726 feet above the water, holding up the two steel cables that anchor the bridge. Inside each of the steel cables are approximately 80,000 miles of wire. Upon completion, the bridge was painted in a colour known as International Orange, because it complements the bridge's surroundings and, more importantly, makes it easier for boats to see it in the thick fog that is often seen hovering over the bay. During its construction,

25 there were many accidents with workers falling. Eleven workers died from these falls, so safety nets were installed under the bridge that ultimately contributed to saving the lives of 19 construction workers, including their foreman, Evan Lambert. The Golden Gate Bridge was finally opened in May 1937 and although not the world's tallest, longest or busiest bridge, it has since been named one of the seven wonders of the modern world.

30 Just after the turn of the 20th century, San Francisco was struck by a devastating earthquake that measured a magnitude of 7.9 on the Richter scale. In excess of 80% of the city was decimated, mainly due to the vast number of devastating fires that broke out. These blazes lasted for several days and over 3000 people lost their lives. Around 300,000 residents out of a total population of 400,000 were displaced and housed in makeshift tents erected in the parks and on the city's beaches. Many residents were still

35 living in these squalid refugee camps more than two years later.

The tiny island nestling in San Francisco Bay – Alcatraz – was once home to America's most notorious prison. The jail was established in August 1934 and housed America's criminals who perennially behaved badly in other less secure prisons. The choppy waters surrounding the island are prone to exceptionally strong currents, thereby making escape virtually impossible. During its 29 years as a prison, it is reported that no inmate successfully escaped from Alcatraz, although there were numerous inmates that tried. A total of 36 prisoners sought to escape – two men twice tried to flee – 23 were caught and returned to jail, six were shot dead and two drowned. Five prisoners are still officially listed as 'missing, presumed drowned'.

40

Carefully read through the passage on the previous page and above and circle the correct answers below.

1 How many years did the Golden Gate Bridge take to construct?

A. Four years

B. Two years

C. Eight years

D. 21 years

2 Which one of the following statements is not true?

A. The Golden Gate Bridge is painted in International Orange.

B. Blazes were to blame for the massive destruction of parts of the city in 1906.

C. The prison on Alcatraz housed persistently problematic prisoners.

D. To this day, horse-drawn cabs are still a fashionable mode of transport in San Francisco.

3 How many of the escapees from Alcatraz officially didn't survive after fleeing the jail?

A. 23 prisoners

B. Six prisoners

C. 13 prisoners

D. Five prisoners

/3

4   What percentage of San Francisco's citizens were forced to seek refuge in temporary accommodation in the wake of the city's catastrophic earthquake in 1906?

A. Approximately 60%

B. Around 75%

C. About 80%

D. Approximately 50%

---

5   Whose design was ultimately accepted for the erection of the Golden Gate Bridge?

A. James Wilkins

B. Michael O'Shaughnessy

C. James Marshall

D. Joseph Strauss

---

6   What action did the authorities take to minimise injuries and fatalities during the construction of the Golden Gate Bridge?

A. They arranged for the construction workers to wear a safety harness.

B. They employed a health and safety team to oversee the building work.

C. They installed safety nets under the bridge.

D. The workers were all supplied with first-aid kits.

---

7   What was the occupation of the man who struck gold in the region in the mid-19th century?

A. He was a carpenter.

B. He was a fisherman.

C. He was a gold prospector.

D. He was an engineer.

/4

8 Which one of the following statements is true?

A. The body of water over which the Golden Gate Bridge crosses is the Pacific Ocean.

B. The Golden Gate Bridge finally opened almost 90 years after the first designs were considered by the San Franciscan authorities.

C. The waters surrounding the island of Alcatraz are surprisingly calm all year round.

D. Alcatraz ceased to operate as a prison facility in the late 1970s.

---

9 According to the text, which accolade has the Golden Gate Bridge earned?

A. It is the longest bridge in the world.

B. It is the world's most photographed suspension bridge.

C. It has the most expensive toll charges in the Western world.

D. It has been designated as one of the seven wonders of the modern world.

---

10 What kind of weather conditions often occur around San Francisco Bay?

A. Heavy snowfall

B. Torrential rain

C. Dense mist

D. Thick clouds

/3

Comprehension 5

London

Strand

The Strand is the street which extends out east from Trafalgar Square.

The Strand has been lined with pubs – or taverns, as they used to be called – since the 15th century. The Duck and Drake Tavern was famous as it was the meeting place for Guy Fawkes and the other men who plotted to blow up the Houses of Parliament in 1605.

In the 18th century, tea houses and coffee shops began to spring up along the Strand and, in 1706, Thomas Twining opened his first shop at number 206 – shortly before becoming the first sole supplier of tea to Queen Anne.

By the 19th century, the Strand had become a very chic and fashionable part of London, and many notable writers, such as Charles Dickens and George Eliot, moved into the area and would often congregate in the ever-popular Nag's Head Tavern. The Rose Tavern was a popular venue for lawyers to meet.

Pioneer of en-suite bathrooms and electric lighting, the lavish Savoy Hotel was built in 1889 on the site of the medieval Savoy Palace. The forecourt of the hotel is the only street in Britain where traffic drives on the right-hand side of the road.

Fleet Street

Fleet Street is one of the major streets in the City of London and is famous for producing newspapers.

Publishing first began in Fleet Street around 1500, which was when William Caxton installed Britain's first printing press and began supplying the legal trade with official documents. Around this time many new taverns opened, and famous playwright William Shakespeare was a regular patron of the Old Mitre Tavern. Later, in early 1702, Britain's first newspaper, The *Daily Courant*, was published in Fleet Street – conveniently placed for Westminster and the City of London, which were the main sources of news.

Soon after came The *Morning Chronicle,* and then The *Daily Express* established itself at number 121. By the early 1900s, Fleet Street was home to the offices of all of the country's major national newspapers.

Ye Old Cheddar Cheese Tavern was the favoured choice of most journalists in Fleet Street and El Vino's wine bar became the favourite place for lawyers to meet.

Trafalgar Square

Trafalgar Square, built around the area formerly known as Charing Cross, commemorates the Battle of Trafalgar, which took place between Britain and the allied fleets of the French and Spanish navies in 1805.

Nelson's Column dominates the Square and is one of London's most famous landmarks. It was built in 1843 and comprises a 5.5m sandstone statue of Lord Horatio Nelson standing on top of a 46m solid granite column. Nelson faces south towards the Admiralty, with The Mall on his right flank.

Trafalgar Square has long been the place for political meetings and rallies.

Every year, in December, a huge Christmas tree is erected in the centre of the square. It has been an annual gift from the people of Norway since World War II. The tree is a token of gratitude for Britain keeping Norway's Prince Olav and the country's government safely exiled in London during the war. The tree is decorated with lights which are switched on in a ceremony 12 days before Christmas Day.

Carefully read through the passage on the previous page and circle the correct answers below.

1 Which countries were involved in a naval battle in 1805?

A. Spain, Italy and France

B. Britain, France and Germany

C. Spain, France and Germany

D. France, Spain and Britain

2 How tall overall is Nelson's Column?

A. 5.5 metres

B. 51.5 metres

C. 46 metres

D. 52.5 metres

3 Who was the British monarch in 1706?

A. King James I

B. Henry VIII

C. Queen Anne

D. Charles II

4 What is unusual about the street outside the Savoy Hotel?

A. It is the only street in Britain where cars do not drive on the left.

B. It is the only street in London where taxis are prohibited.

C. It is the only street in Britain not to have any street lights.

D. It is the only street in London not to have any road markings.

/4

5 Which two pubs were very popular with lawyers?

A. The Duck and Drake and the Rose Tavern

B. The Old Mitre Tavern and the Duck and Drake

C. The Nag's Head and Ye Old Cheddar Cheese Tavern

D. El Vino's wine bar and the Rose Tavern

6 Which was Britain's first newspaper to be published?

A. *The Morning Chronicle*

B. *The Daily Courant*

C. *The Daily Express*

D. *The Times*

7 What was the area around Trafalgar Square once known as?

A. Charing Cross

B. Fleet Street

C. The Edgeware Road

D. Maida Vale

8 On which date are the Christmas tree lights in Trafalgar Square turned on?

A. On 15 December

B. On 18 December

C. On 13 December

D. On Christmas Eve

/4

9 Which one of the following statements is true?

A. Britain's first printing press was operating in 1205.

B. The Savoy was the second luxury London hotel to offer en-suite bathrooms.

C. Pubs were once known as tea rooms.

D. Nelson's Column is situated to the left of The Mall.

---

10 Which one of the following statements is true?

A. Guy Fawkes and his co-conspirators used to congregate in the Nag's Head.

B. The Norwegian government took sanctuary in London during World War I.

C. Britain's first newspaper was published in 1500.

D. Trafalgar Square is located to the west of the Strand.

/2

Comprehension 6

July 20, 1937

OBITUARY

AMELIA EARHART, A PILOT OF COURAGE AND SKILL

Hope has now been officially abandoned that Miss Amelia Earhart could have survived her last adventurous flight, after having been missing for over a fortnight. Miss Earhart left Miami, Florida, on June 1st to fly around the world from west to east, with Fred Noonan as her navigator. Her machine was a Lockheed Electra. She arrived at Dumdum airport, Calcutta, on June 17, having completed more than half of her journey. From there she flew to the Australian port of Darwin, arriving in the early hours of June 28. Three days later, Miss Earhart took off for Howland Island which was the most hazardous part of her itinerary. Although mayday signals are reported to have been received from her, she has never been seen again, and prolonged searches by sea and air have failed to discover any traces of her or her plane.

Amelia Earhart was born in Kansas on July 24, 1898. During the war she served with the Canadian Red Cross, and afterwards studied at Columbia University. She then learned to fly, but her chosen occupation in life was social welfare work with children in Boston.

Miss Earhart was 30 years old when she first crossed the Atlantic by air. Mrs Amy Guest, wife of the former Secretary of State for Air, financed the flight to the tune of £8000, and had originally intended to fly in the plane herself. However, after much thought she decided to give up her place to Miss Earhart.

The three-engined aircraft was fitted with floats as an extra safety feature and was aptly named *Friendship*.

Miss Earhart – with her pilot and mechanic – departed from Newfoundland on June 17 1928 and 21 hours later touched down in South Wales.

It was after her marriage – on February 7, 1931 – to George Putnam, of the publishing house, that she was able to realise her ambition of flying the Atlantic as a solo pilot, and famously she was to become the first woman to do so. She was quite frank about her feelings. She did not profess that the flight would do any good to anyone. "I did it really for fun," she said, "not to set up any records or anything like that."

This time she chose a fast single-engined aeroplane and on May 20, 1932, she took off from the airport at Harbour Grace, Newfoundland. After 13 hours she made landfall in the town of Donegal, in the west of Ireland. Miss Earhart had made the fastest Atlantic crossing to date. She met with several difficulties with her instruments during her flight, but she was an experienced pilot and doubtless her previous crossing stood her in good stead. When she was still four hours out, one section of the engine exhaust began to leak.

At the same time she met bad weather and had to begin blind flying, and soon after her altimeter failed her. Miss Earhart told our Aeronautical reporter that she then climbed up into the clouds until the tachometer froze, "and then I knew I couldn't be near the sea." She thought she went up to 12,000ft., but ice began to form on the wings and the clouds were still heavy above her. Meanwhile the intense heat around the leaking exhaust began to melt away the metal. She looked over at it and wished she hadn't, as she saw flames coming out, and it worried her all night. Other parts began to work loose, the plane began to shake and the engine 'began to run rough'. Petrol leaked into the cockpit from the petrol gauge, and there was the danger that the fumes would reach the exhaust and explode.

At last she guessed she had made Ireland, but could not be sure, so she turned north until she saw the hills above the mouth of the River Foyle. Following the railway track, she made an almost perfect landing on a small farm near Londonderry, and was warmly greeted and entertained by the farmer and his wife.

When Miss Earhart travelled on to London the next day, she was met by her adoring, proud husband and a huge crowd of well-wishers.

Carefully read through the passage on the previous page and circle the correct answers below.

1 For how long had Amelia Earhart been missing before she was presumed to be dead?

A. More than two weeks

B. Exactly one week

C. Over a month

D. Three days

2 On which date did Amelia Earhart start out for Howland Island?

A. 30 June

B. 17 June

C. 2 July

D. 1 July

3 In which country is the port of Darwin located?

A. India

B. America

C. Australia

D. China

4 Who funded Amelia Earhart's first Atlantic flight?

A. George Putnam

B. Amy Guest

C. Fred Noonan

D. The US government

/4

5 What inspired Amelia Earhart to attempt a solo flight across the Atlantic Ocean?

A. She wanted to break the world record for solo flying.

B. She thought she would find the experience amusing and entertaining.

C. She wanted to be the first woman to fly across the Atlantic.

D. She desperately wanted to be famous.

---

6 How many engines did the aircraft have in which Amelia Earhart completed her solo flight across the Atlantic?

A. Three

B. Four

C. Just one

D. Two

---

7 How was Amelia Earhart able to overcome the problems with her plane on her solo flight?

A. Her vast experience as an aviator meant that she was able to react to, and work around, the difficulties.

B. She sent out mayday messages to get help.

C. She shut down the power and glided for the rest of the flight.

D. She landed on a small island and set about repairing the faults.

---

8 How did the Irish farmer react when Miss Earhart landed in one of his fields?

A. He and his wife were furious as Miss Earhart had ruined most of his potato crop.

B. He was stunned and wasn't at all sure what was happening.

C. He was frightened as he thought it may be an enemy aircraft.

D. He was charming and welcoming.

/4

9 Which one of the following statements is true?

A. Miss Earhart could not always be certain of her exact altitude during her solo flight.

B. Miss Earhart worked in a publishing house when she wasn't flying planes.

C. There were three other people on the plane when Miss Earhart first crossed the Atlantic.

D. Components of Miss Earhart's plane caught fire minutes before she landed in Ireland.

---

10 Which one of the following statements is not true?

A. Amelia Earhart followed a railway line to guide her in to land in Ireland.

B. Amelia Earhart had been married for less than two years before she triumphed on her solo flight.

C. Amelia Earhart was born in Calcutta.

D. Amelia Earhart attended university after the war was over.

/2

Comprehension 7

Houses for Sale

Albert Close, Stroud   £799,000

Located on the north side of Stroud with good access to both the town centre and the M5 motorway, Albert Close is situated on the edge of the prestigious Slad Estate with far-reaching views over the Cotswolds. Number 16 is a newly constructed, detached property which has been designed by multi-award-winning architects. This contemporary home offers bespoke living in a well-proportioned space. The accommodation briefly comprises: spacious, open-plan kitchen/dining/family room and three double bedrooms all with en-suite bathrooms. To the front of the property is a large gravelled driveway, and to the rear is a beautifully landscaped, south-facing garden. The house benefits from gas central heating with energy-efficient underfloor heating throughout the ground-floor rooms.

Chimney's End, Bredon   £795,000

Dating back to the early 17th century, this Grade II listed detached residence retains a wealth of fine period features, including a Tudor stone arched fireplace. The house is set in beautifully landscaped gardens, with an apple orchard and countryside views. The principal house comprises a large living room, music room, dining room, conservatory, study and fully fitted kitchen. On the first floor there are four double bedrooms – one of which boasts a stunning walk-in wardrobe – and three further bedrooms on the second floor. There are three bathrooms and there is ample storage space throughout. The latest addition to this splendid property – accessed via the kitchen – is a large separate living space with its own dining room, lounge, fitted kitchen and bedroom with an en-suite. There is ample off-road parking for several vehicles and a large, double garage. Highly recommended.

Taylor's End, Alderton   £895,000

A magnificent detached period-style former farmhouse with many character features and beautifully restored accommodation. Taylor's End enjoys far-reaching views. Discreetly positioned in the easily accessible village of Alderton, the ground floor comprises three reception rooms, a refitted kitchen/ breakfast room, utility room and a cloakroom. The first floor features a 40m² master bedroom with en-suite bathroom, four further double bedrooms and three further bath/shower rooms. The rear gardens back onto fields and at the southern end, a covered terrace serves as an excellent barbecue area. The charming village of Alderton lies just four miles to the north of Winchcombe, seven miles from Tewkesbury and ten miles from Cheltenham. There is a village post office and shop, a village school, the popular Gardener's Arms public house and the church of St Margaret of Antioch. The village contains a pleasant mix of both stone and red brick properties, as well as earlier wattle and daub thatched houses. The property's gravel driveway can easily accommodate up to six vehicles and there is also a double garage. The property boasts two garden sheds and stabling for up to three ponies.

Cleeve House, Cheltenham £810,000

A substantial and stunning detached residence, occupying an elevated plot on Cleeve Hill with stunning views towards the Malvern and Welsh hills. The property has been lovingly updated by its current owners, with its 1930s heritage being extremely well-maintained. The accommodation on the ground floor includes a living room, formal dining room, large study, and a kitchen with patio doors opening out into the conservatory. On the second floor is the family bathroom, a separate WC and three spacious double bedrooms. To the rear is a beautifully maintained garden incorporating a charming, shallow brook. There is a large patio to enjoy the ever-changing sunsets. The patio leads to the central lawn with well-stocked borders which in turn drop down into an established orchard. The garden isn't the only amazing outside space on offer: Cleeve Hill, just across the road, offers round-the-year golf. Walking, mountain biking and horse riding are also available locally.

Must be seen.

Court Road, Cheltenham £655,999

An imposing five-bedroom detached house set with substantial gardens in a highly sought after tree-lined road, within easy reach of good local amenities. Its well-proportioned accommodation, though now in need of updating, retains a wealth of character features and comprises on the upper ground floor: a generous entrance hall, cloakroom, sitting room, dining room, study and a conservatory. Below there is a kitchen, family room, walk-in larder, wine cellar, laundry room and a cloakroom. The upper two floors provide five double bedrooms, two bathrooms and another cloakroom. Further benefits of this fine residence include a surprisingly large garden in the region of a third of an acre, and off-road parking. The property also benefits from its location within the catchment area of an outstanding secondary school.

Carefully read through the passage on the previous page and above and circle the correct answers below.

1 Which property has a small stream running through its garden?

A. Taylor's End

B. Cleeve House

C. Chimney's End

D. The property in Albert Close

2 What is the difference in price between the least and most expensive properties?

A. £219,001

B. £349,001

C. £339,001

D. £239,001

/2

3 Which one of the following statements is true?

A. The property in Court Road is the only house that is not detached.

B. The property in Stroud is the most recently built home.

C. Cleeve House was originally constructed in the early 19th century.

D. Taylor's End has a newly built separate living space on the ground floor.

4 Which property was constructed between the years 1600 and 1650?

A. Chimney's End

B. Taylor's End

C. Cleeve House

D. The property in Court Road

5 In which direction does the garden face at 16 Albert Close?

A. West

B. South-east

C. South

D. North

6 Which one of the following phrases best describes the village of Alderton?

A. Slightly overcrowded and expensive

B. Delightful, with an excellent range of local amenities

C. Spoilt and overrun with cars visiting the Gardener's Arms

D. Friendly, but the trees and hedgerows are somewhat overgrown

/4

7 Which one of the following statements is true?

   A. Cleeve House has the highest asking price.

   B. The property in Court Road has three floors.

   C. Chimney's End has a total of four bedrooms.

   D. Winchcombe lies four miles to the south of Alderton.

---

8 Which one of the following statements is not true?

   A. Taylor's End is fewer than a dozen miles from Cheltenham.

   B. Cleeve Hill is ideal for mountain biking.

   C. The property in Court Road is contemporary and fresh.

   D. Chimney's End boasts a curved stone fireplace.

---

9 How many of the properties have an orchard?

   A. Two

   B. Three

   C. One

   D. Four

---

10 Which of the following statements is not true?

   A. The most expensive property used to be located on a farm.

   B. The least expensive property has two bathrooms.

   C. The third most expensive property benefits from underfloor heating.

   D. The most expensive property has an apple orchard.

/4

Comprehension 8

Victorian Child Labour

In any Victorian town, it was not difficult to determine who was rich and who was poor. The children from more affluent homes were well nourished, dressed smartly and attended school or were educated at home. Poor children were thin, constantly hungry and they wore ragged, dirty clothes. The majority of poor children had no shoes and they would begin their working lives between the tender ages of five

5 and eight.

Anne is nine years old and the third youngest of nine children in her family. Anne has just started working six and a half days a week in a textile mill at the end of her street. Her main job is to clean the machines at the mill. Anne's bosses refuse to pause the machines for cleaning and she is frightened that she will become injured as she clambers under the huge machinery all day. Many children in Anne's mill

10 have lost limbs and some have even been killed, so she is petrified every single day.

Ted is 22 years old and he has worked at the matchstick factory since he was six years old. He rises daily at 5am and has a meal of bread and jam before walking to the factory to begin his 13-hour shift at 6am. As a matchstick maker, Ted works in a crowded, badly ventilated room, dipping tiny wooden sticks into phosphorus and sulphur. The fumes from the mixture are noxious but Ted has no choice but to inhale

15 the poisonous gases. Often his gums and jaw will swell up, leaving Ted in agony.

Lizzie is 12 years old and has been employed as an under-housemaid for two years. Her day begins at 6.30am every day when she cleans the grates and lights all the fires in the three-storey London home where she lives and works. She then scrubs the floor in the scullery and boils the water for the master's daily bath. Lizzie spends an hour each morning making all the beds – including her own bed on the top

20 floor of the house – and sweeping the bedroom floors. After a 20-minute break for lunch, she turns her attention to cleaning the brasses and gas lamps. In the afternoons, Lizzie sits down with the sewing box and darns any clothes or sheets that might need mending. At 4pm sharp, Lizzie joins the other servants below stairs for tea, which is usually a simple meal of bread and cheese. She spends her evenings clearing away and washing the dishes after the master and mistress have dined. She finally retires at 11pm and falls

25 asleep almost instantly because she is exhausted.

Wilf has seven brothers and two sisters, and works hard as a chimney sweep in London. The practice of using children as 'climbing boys' – as they were known – began after the Great Fire of London when new building laws were introduced; fireplaces had to be built with much narrower chimneys and had to be cleaned regularly. Wilf seldom sees his parents and siblings as he was purchased from his family by

30 a master sweep when he was just four years old. Wilf has to crawl up chimneys using just his knees and elbows. He uses a brush to dislodge the soot which falls down on top of him, and then he slides down the chimney and collects the soot pile for his master, who sells it. Wilf receives no wages for this hard, dangerous work and he is dreading the time when he has grown too big to climb chimneys as he knows that he will then be on the streets.

35 Alf is just eight years old and has perhaps the worst job of all; this is his first year working in a coal mine, and his working conditions are pitiful. Between 1791 and 1850, around one in three eight-year-old working-class boys in England were forced to go out to work. Alf enters the coal mine through a shaft at 2am every day and spends the next 12 hours working as a 'putter'; he pushes trucks of coal along the tunnels in the mine. The coal mine is a very dark place in which to work as the only source of light

40 comes from a few small candles. Alf knows that the mine is at real risk of flooding or collapsing and that the spark from a pickaxe could cause trapped gases to explode.

Carefully read through the passage on the previous page and above and circle the correct answers below.

1 How many older siblings does Anne have?

A. Nine

B. Eight

C. Six

D. Seven

---

2 Who started working from the youngest age?

A. Wilf

B. Ted

C. Anne

D. Lizzie

---

3 How were impoverished children instantly recognisable during Victorian times?

A. Their clothes were generally tattered.

B. They were often skinny.

C. They frequently wore no footwear.

D. All of the above

/3

4 Find three adjectives in Alf's story?

A. worst, only, every

B. small, dark, trapped

C. first, real, forced

D. pushes, perhaps, pickaxe

---

5 Which one of the following statements is true?

A. Lizzie sits down to tea in the servants' hall at about 3.45pm.

B. Anne is blissfully unaware of the fatalities at the mill where she works.

C. Ted feels lucky to work in an airy environment.

D. Alf finishes his shift at 14:00.

---

6 What was the popular name for child chimney sweeps in Victorian England?

A. Chimney boys

B. Climbing boys

C. Apprentice sweeps

D. Master sweeps

---

7 Which one of the following statements is true?

A. Ted cycles to work at 5.30am every morning.

B. Lizzie's sleeping quarters are on the ground floor in her employer's house.

C. Anne works from Mondays to Sundays every week.

D. Alf has to feel his way along the mine as there is no light in the tunnels.

/4

8 How long does Lizzie have for her daily lunch break?

A. A mere 20 minutes

B. One hour exactly

C. She is not permitted to pause for lunch.

D. Just 10 minutes

---

9 What are Wilf's wages from chimney sweeping?

A. Ten shillings per week

B. Five shillings each week

C. Nothing

D. Just a shilling every week

---

10 What concerns Alf when he is working in the coal mine?

A. He knows that the tunnels could become submerged with water.

B. He is acutely aware that the tunnels could collapse at any time.

C. He worries about an explosion caused by gases.

D. All of the above

/3

The Hermitage Museum

With almost three million exhibits on display, the Hermitage Museum, in Russia's cultural capital city of St Petersburg, is the world's second largest. The museum was established during the reign of Catherine the Great, who was Empress of Russia from 1762 to 1796. The Hermitage Museum houses the world's largest collection of paintings, including priceless pieces by the Dutch baroque artist Rembrandt, the Italian
5　Renaissance master Leonardo da Vinci and the great Dutch post-Impressionist painter Van Gogh.

One of the museum's most captivating exhibits is the Peacock Clock – crafted by the eminent London goldsmith James Cox, who was commissioned to design the clock in 1777. The solid gold clock features an owl, a rooster and a peacock, in addition to a squirrel, a fox and a mushroom. Every Wednesday at precisely 8pm, the clock chimes, and when it does so, first the owl turns its head, then the magnificent
10　peacock elegantly turns its neck to the left and raises its tail purposefully before fanning its stunning plume of feathers. This astonishing spectacle ends with the eerie crowing of the rooster.

Perhaps the most unusual feature of the Hermitage Museum is its small army of pampered cats, which are themselves a major tourist attraction. The priceless treasures of the museum are at constant risk of damage from rodent activity, so a total of 75 cats are kept by the Hermitage to protect the works of art. By
15　day, the cats sleep in the basement on special beds balanced on the building's central heating pipes, and hunt by night. They have been guarding the contents of the museum for over 250 years.

The cats first appeared during the reign of Peter the Great's daughter, Empress Elizabeth, who was crowned on 6 May 1742 and ruled until her death on Christmas Day 1762. Prior to the Hermitage buildings being transformed into a museum, the Empress had become so disgruntled with the hundreds
20　of rodents running through her Tsarist palace that she introduced a new law. This law ordered that the very best vermin-catching cats were to be rounded up immediately and sent to her to rid the building of the pests.

Nowadays, there aren't enough rodents to provide for all the cats' nutritional requirements, so in order to supplement the cats' diets, there is a small kitchen in which two dedicated chefs prepare tasty meals of
25　fish, meat, cereals and milk each day. Food and water bowls can be spotted all around the galleries in the museum. There are also three busy volunteer workers who tend to the cats' every need, and there is even a little, yet well-equipped, vet's surgery and operating theatre for treating illnesses and injuries.

When the time comes for a cat to 'retire' from their duties at the Hermitage Museum, they are quickly replaced by new stray or abandoned cats. St Petersburg city residents race to offer new homes to the
30　cats, as when they leave the museum, each feline is issued with its own 'Hermitage passport' – with its photograph inside – and a special 'Hermitage certificate'. Both documents give the veteran cats a certain amount of kudos and make them very popular and much sought-after little creatures.

Carefully read through the passage on the previous page and circle the correct answers below.

1 To which species of animal do rats belong?

   A. Felines

   B. Rodents

   C. Primates

   D. Carnivores

---

2 How many people look after the cats at the museum?

   A. Just one – the museum caretaker

   B. Two busy volunteers

   C. Five – three volunteers and two chefs

   D. None, they are strays and can look after themselves.

---

3 Which one of the following statements is true?

   A. The Hermitage is the largest museum in the world.

   B. Visitors to the Hermitage Museum generally find the cats tiresome.

   C. Empress Elizabeth was the niece of Peter the Great.

   D. There are facilities for sick and wounded cats to be treated at the Hermitage.

---

4 What was the Hermitage before it became a museum?

   A. The headquarters of the Russian army

   B. One of the Russian Tsar's palaces

   C. A disused Russian government building

   D. A huge art gallery

/4

5 For how long did Empress Elizabeth rule Russia?

A. Over 20 years and seven months

B. Just fewer than 20 years and six months

C. Longer than 30 years and seven months

D. Exactly 20 years

---

6 '...crafted by the eminent London goldsmith James Cox...' (lines 6 and 7)

What does the word 'eminent' mean in this context?

A. Wealthy

B. Fortunate

C. Distinguished

D. Popular

---

7 How many winged creatures feature in the Peacock Clock display?

A. Six

B. Seven

C. Three

D. Five

---

8 Which one of the following statements is true?

A. St Petersburg is considered to be the country's capital city for the arts and culture.

B. The Peacock Clock chimes daily at exactly 8 o'clock in the morning.

C. Leonardo da Vinci was an Italian artist in the baroque style.

D. Catherine the Great ruled for a total of 36 years.

/4

The Diaries of Florence Nightingale

Tuesday 25 July 1837. Today I was ambling through the gardens at Embley when I suddenly began to hear voices in my head. 'Florence,' the voice urged, 'you have been put on this earth to heal the sick, this is to be your vocation and you are to pursue it with all your heart and soul.' This evening, after dinner, I dared to ask Papa if I could have his blessing if I chose to become a nurse. He stated clearly that he would never
5   countenance such a proposal.

Monday 12 May 1851. Today, on the occasion of my 31st birthday, my father hosted a dinner party at our London home and the guests included Sir Edwin Chadwick and the Earl of Shaftsbury; both fine gentlemen who are staunch advocates of social reform. The menfolk conversed about the appalling conditions that are prevalent both in hospitals and workhouses and the urgent need for change. Another
10   of the guests was Sir Harry Verney, who this evening asked for my hand in marriage. I declined his proposal because I am resolute in my determination not to live a life of domesticity. I do not wish to merely marry and raise children as Papa and Mama would wish.

Tuesday 20 May 1851. It has become apparent that I am a disappointment to Papa and Mama who steadfastly refuse to accept my wishes; Papa has sought to prevent my applications for nursing training
15   here in England. Today I have resolved to further my nursing ambitions and attempt to arrange training overseas.

Tuesday 15 July 1851. After many telegrams between myself and a medical institution in Germany, I am delighted to hear that I have been accepted to undergo nursing training. My passage leaves on 25th of this month and I will be away for a couple of months. I have prayed that Papa and Mama may give me their
20   blessing, but it has not been forthcoming and I may depart for Europe on bad terms with my beloved family. Even my sister Frances could not hide her disapproval.

Monday 12 September 1853. I have returned to London after my training and I have begun nursing in Harley Street. I have been appointed Nursing Superintendent and my duties are to nurse dying women; mostly retired governesses. I am also to be in charge of all of the finances at the institution. I have taken
25   rooms in Pall Mall to be near my work.

Tuesday 28th March, 1854. News has reached us today that Britain and France are in a state of war with Russia. The *London Times* is reporting that fighting is taking place on the Crimean peninsula and that there have been heavy casualties.

Thursday 12 October 1854. This evening I was honoured to have attended a private meeting with
30   Sidney Herbert, the Secretary of War. He has informed me that fighting has intensified in the Crimea and has asked me to urgently oversee the recruitment of at least three dozen trained nurses to care for wounded soldiers in the military hospital at Scutari, in the Ottoman Empire.

Saturday 4 November 1854. After an arduous passage across France, my party of nurses and I have arrived in Scutari and, upon inspection of the facilities here, we are appalled. Soldiers are being housed
35   in buildings that are overrun with vermin and there is a distinct lack of even the most basic equipment or medicines. It is evident that most of the patients are suffering from infections caused by the lack of hygiene rather than from wounds sustained on the battlefields. Our work here is clear and we must

now work tirelessly to thoroughly disinfect as best we can. We need to urgently improve the sanitary arrangements, scrub the linen and soldiers' clothing and establish food kitchens to properly feed the men.

40 **Monday 15 January 1855.** I am unable to delay a moment longer; today I corresponded with Lord Raglan, the British Army commander. I pray that, by depicting the dire deficiencies in the medical facilities at Scutari, help will be forthcoming in the form of adequate provision of trained medical staff. This will assist with reducing the appalling mortality rate that I am recording in my daily nursing journal.

45 **Monday 1 January 1856.** Thankfully, our great Queen has mobilised resources and we have received sufficient donations from the public back in Britain to enable the procurement of medical equipment and, most importantly, employ workmen to thoroughly cleanse the drains.

Sunday 30 March 1856. Our prayers have been answered as we hear news of the cessation of hostilities; we are to return to Britain forthwith.

50 **Friday 4 April 1856.** Upon my return to my rooms in London, I am greatly privileged to have received a telegram from Her Majesty Queen Victoria – I am to be summoned to Buckingham Palace for a private meeting with our monarch to discuss my work in the Crimea. I am humbled to learn that reports of our labours have been published in all the major newspapers and that I am now a well-known figure throughout the whole of Britain.

55 **Wednesday 16 April 1856.** Her Majesty informed me today that the country had decided to bestow a large sum of money upon me. These funds have been amassed from donations raised by the public up and down the land. I propose to use the funds to establish a school in which to train nurses.

Thursday 24 June 1858. Today, I was Matron of Honour at my sister Frances's wedding. I am no longer estranged from my family; they have declared that they are now proud of me and my achievements.
60 Frances became Lady Verney today and will now live at Claydon House with Harry.

Monday 9 July 1860. Today, I attended the official opening of the Nightingale Training School for Nurses. I pray that my time in nursing will inspire more women to join such a caring profession.

Carefully read through the passage on the previous page and above and circle the correct answers below.

1 What aspirations did Florence Nightingale's parents have for their daughter?

A. They had ambitions for her to become a surgeon.

B. They wanted her to become a teacher.

C. They would have been happy for her just to marry and have a family.

D. They would have liked her to become a children's governess.

/1

2 What were Florence Nightingale's primary concerns upon her arrival in Scutari?

A. The buildings were infested with rats.

B. The conditions were filthy.

C. There were inadequate supplies of medicines and equipment.

D. All of the above

---

3 Which one of the following statements is true?

A. Florence's initial nursing training took place in Italy.

B. The Crimean War ended in the autumn of 1856.

C. Florence was based in Scutari for 17 months in total.

D. The government tasked Florence Nightingale with recruiting over 100 nurses.

---

4 What did most of the patients in the Harley Street clinic have in common?

A. The majority of the patients had had a career as a governess.

B. Most of them were injured soldiers.

C. They were mostly retired teachers.

D. Most of them were immensely wealthy.

---

5 In which national newspaper was the outbreak of the Crimean War reported?

A. The *Daily Telegraph*

B. The *London Times*

C. The *Daily Mirror*

D. The *Daily Mail*

/4

6 How old was Florence Nightingale on the occasion of her sister's wedding?

A. 37 years old

B. 48 years old

C. 38 years old

D. 42 years old

---

7 Which one of the following statements is true?

A. Florence Nightingale never received a proposal of marriage during her entire lifetime.

B. Florence was honoured to be asked to be her sister's chief bridesmaid at her wedding.

C. Sidney Herbert was the British Army commander at the time of the Crimean War.

D. Britain and France were allies in the Crimean War against Russia.

---

8 Which one of the following statements is not true?

A. Florence's parents gave her their support when she embarked on her initial training.

B. Florence Nightingale relocated near to Harley Street in the autumn of 1853.

C. The Nightingale Training School for Nurses was entirely funded by public donations.

D. Florence Nightingale was inspired to help the sick when she heard voices in her head.

/3

Comprehension 11

Amazing Animals of Africa

Zambia's Kasanka National Park features picturesque lakes, rivers and lush woodlands. The park serves as an important conservation area, providing sanctuary for endangered species. These include blue monkeys, cheetahs, African wild dogs and the ever-reclusive sitatunga, a swamp-dwelling species of antelope.

5   However, Kasanka is most famous for the bewitching spectacle of ten million fruit bats migrating to the park in the last three months of the year. The straw-coloured mammals target the fruits of the forests which have ripened and are at their most abundant. Scientists have recently attached navigation equipment to some of the bats which indicate that they fly from the Democratic Republic of Congo, a country situated 1000km to the north-west. The fruit bats – who, contrary to popular belief, are not
10 blind, but can in fact see three times as well as humans – can grow to have a wingspan of 85cm and can weigh up to 1.6kg. The mammals spend their days suspended from the branches of the trees of the forest before venturing out at dusk to gorge on bananas, peaches, dates, figs and sometimes mangoes. They are capable of devouring twice their own body weight during a single night's feasting.

North-west of Zambia lie Kenya and the Mara River, which is the scene for one of nature's most
15 spectacular sights and events: the annual mass migration of one million wildebeest, along with hundreds of thousands of gazelles and zebras. The ungulates are driven to crossing the treacherous, crocodile-infested waters of the Mara in order to seek fresh water and grazing pasture as their natural habitat in the Serengeti region of Tanzania becomes arid during the summer months. As they make their arduous, perilous journey to fresh pastures, lions, leopards, jackals, cheetahs and hyena lie in wait, hoping for
20 rich pickings. As they do so, vultures swirl ominously overhead, hoping to dine on the remnants of the carcasses that the predatory carnivores leave behind. When the rains return to the Serengeti, the wildebeest must set out on the hazardous return journey home.

At the southernmost tip of the continent there is the phenomenon of the Great Sardine Run, which takes place annually from May to July. Sardines – also known as pilchards – are small, silvery fish which live in
25 huge shoals in the world's oceans. During the Great Sardine Run, millions of sardines migrate in massive shoals to the cooler waters of the Cape. The sardines endure a perilous journey; they have numerous predators, the deadliest of which is man – anglers stalk the progress of the sardines by flying low over the ocean in light aircraft, and when they spot a huge shoal of sardines, they lower huge nets into the sea and encircle the fish. They then trawl their brimming nets ashore and gather up their mammoth catch.
30 Underwater, the sardines are under attack from sea predators such as huge pods of dolphins who trail the tiny fish all the way up the coast. Sharks, greedy gannets and gulls are also a danger.

Female green sea turtles lay their eggs on land and regularly lay over a hundred eggs in one nest. At birth, a baby green sea turtle measures a mere 5cm in length, but as adults can grow to 1.5 metres. As soon as it has been born, the baby green sea turtle's first task is a Herculean one; they must navigate their way into
35 the sea as swiftly as possible. It is an amazing spectacle to witness the sight of thousands of baby turtles clumsily scurrying through the sand on their first perilous journey to the safety of the Atlantic Ocean. They must avoid numerous predators such as crabs and birds. Once they have reached the water, they will thrive, and their diet for the first few weeks of life will mostly consist of small crabs and jellyfish. As they begin to mature, the green sea turtles become vegetarians but can subsist on plankton and seaweed.

Carefully read through the passage on the previous page and circle the correct answers below.

1 Which species of predatory bird are a danger to the wildebeest as they make their arduous journey north-west?

A. Gannets

B. Herons

C. Vultures

D. Gulls

2 How much fruit is a fruit bat capable of consuming in a single night?

A. Over five kilograms

B. In excess of three kilograms

C. As much as ten kilograms

D. Over 15 kilograms

3 For what reason do sardines migrate north in the summer?

A. They are searching for cooler water.

B. They are migrating in order to breed.

C. They are looking for less-polluted waters.

D. They are driven by their need for fresh sources of food.

4 Where is Zambia located in relation to Kenya?

A. It is north-west of Kenya.

B. It is south of Kenya.

C. It is south-east of Kenya.

D. It is north of Kenya.

/4

5 Which one of the following statements is true?

A. Sardines are under threat from humans.

B. The sitatunga is a very rare species of rodent.

C. The Mara River is situated in the Democratic Republic of Congo.

D. The collective noun for a group of sardines is a pod.

---

6 To which family of animals do zebras, gazelles and wildebeest belong?

A. Cetaceans

B. Primates

C. Marsupials

D. Ungulates

---

7 Which one of the following statements is true?

A. Sardines are sometimes referred to as herrings.

B. Fruit bats have extremely poor eyesight and rely on echolocation to guide them.

C. Cheetahs are classified as an endangered species.

D. Green sea turtles begin their lives as vegetarians.

---

8 How many times larger will a green sea turtle grow from birth to an adult turtle?

A. 25 times

B. 30 times

C. 20 times

D. 15 times

/4

Thomas Cook

Thomas Cook was once one of the world's best-known names in travel, and its founder can be said to have invented modern tourism. He was born on 22 November 1808 in Leicester and was the only child born to John and Elizabeth Cook. When Thomas was just four years old his father died, which meant that Thomas had to leave school at the tender age of ten and find work so he could support his mother.
5 He initially found a job as a gardener's apprentice and later he became a carpenter.

By the time he was 20, Cook was married with a son of his own. He was a deeply religious man and believed that most Victorian social problems were due to excessive alcohol consumption and that the everyday lives of working-class people could be very greatly improved if they drank less alcohol and became better educated. Cook realised that the recent advent of rail travel and the power of the railways
10 could enable many thousands of people to experience travel for the very first time. Cook was convinced that travel would widen their horizons.

Cook organised his first railway excursion in 1841, when he escorted 50 travellers on a day trip from Leicester to Derby. The trip – which cost one shilling – was a huge success and Cook went on to organise dozens of trips between many English towns over the next few years. More and more people
15 booked the excursions and by the end of the 1840s, Cook had taken more than 10,000 people on his popular trips.

By the end of 1850, having already visited Wales, Scotland and Ireland, Cook began to contemplate trips to Europe, the United States and the Middle East. Such thoughts had to be postponed, however, when Sir Joseph Paxton, architect of the Crystal Palace, persuaded Cook to devote himself to bringing
20 workers from Yorkshire and the Midlands to London for the Great Exhibition which was being held the following year. This he did with great enthusiasm, rarely spending a night at home between June and October, and he even produced a newspaper, *Cook's Exhibition Herald and Excursion Advertiser*, in order to promote his tours. By the end of the season, Cook had escorted 150,000 people to London.

In 1855, an International Exhibition was to be held in Paris for the first time and Thomas Cook
25 received dozens of enquiries from would-be travellers. He planned the journey to France with close attention to detail, and in June, he departed with 100 enthusiastic fellow travellers on his first-ever trip to Europe.

Building on his successes in Europe, Thomas made an exploratory trip to North America in 1865. He devised a series of tours covering 4000 miles of railways. The pinnacle of his career, however, came in
30 September 1872 when, at the age of 63, he departed from Leicester on a tour of the world that would keep him away from home for almost eight months. It had long been his ambition to travel 'to Egypt via China', but such a trip only became practicable at the end of 1869 following the opening of the Suez Canal. Cook and his small party of 40 crossed the Atlantic by steamship and made their way through the United States from New York to San Francisco by rail. They then sailed the Pacific to Japan, then
35 across the Inland Sea to China, and afterwards visited Singapore, Ceylon and India. Leaving Bombay, they crossed the Indian Ocean and then the Red Sea into Cairo, from where most of the party travelled back to London. Thomas himself, however, set off on an extended tour of Egypt and Palestine, finally returning home via Turkey, Greece, Italy and France after an absence of 222 days.

Carefully read through the passage on the previous page and circle the correct answers below.

1 How much was the fare on Thomas Cook's initial railway excursion?

A. One pound

B. Two shillings

C. One shilling

D. Five shillings

2 In which year did the Great Exhibition take place?

A. 1851

B. 1850

C. 1840

D. 1855

3 How did Thomas Cook think that travel would benefit working-class Victorians?

A. He thought that they would enjoy drinking in other towns.

B. He was convinced they would enjoy visits to the seaside.

C. He was sure that his travellers would make new friends on the train.

D. He thought that travel would broaden their minds.

4 How did Cook publicise his tours to the Great Exhibition?

A. He published his own newspaper and placed advertisements in its pages.

B. He advertised them on the radio.

C. He stuck posters up on the windows of his house.

D. He walked the streets of Leicester distributing leaflets.

/4

5 How long did Cook's first round-the-world trip take?

A. Six months exactly

B. Over seven months

C. 12 months

D. 18 months

6 Which sea flows into Cairo, the Egyptian capital?

A. The Inland Sea

B. The Indian Ocean

C. The Red Sea

D. The Atlantic Ocean

7 Which one of the following statements is true?

A. Thomas Cook was in his late 60s when he embarked on his first world tour.

B. Thomas Cook had just one sibling, a younger brother.

C. Over a hundred curious travellers accompanied Cook on his first trip to Derby.

D. The Suez Canal was first opened in 1869.

8 Which one of the following statements is true?

A. Thomas Cook's first round-the-world trip set off from London.

B. Thomas Cook worked down a coal mine before he started his travel company.

C. International Exhibitions had been taking place every year since 1845.

D. The Crystal Palace was designed by Joseph Paxton.

/4

Comprehension 13

The Longest Train Journey in the World

Our Trans-Siberian Express train tours between Moscow and Vladivostok take a leisurely two weeks. By the time our journey concludes, we will have passed through eight time zones, a third of the world's total, and travelled an incredible distance of 11,000 kilometres through Russia and Mongolia.

Here are six of the highlights from the itinerary for this year.

- **Days 1 & 2:** Our amazing adventure begins in Moscow and we will meet at the Kremlin – the spiritual, historical and political heart of the city – where we will have the opportunity to view the treasures of the ruling Tsars in the Armoury Chamber. We will also visit Red Square, an iconic symbol of Russia's former military and political might. The next morning, we will board the *Golden Eagle* Trans-Siberian Express for our exciting 12-night adventure to Vladivostok.

- **Days 3 & 4:** Our first port of call on our journey will be Yekaterinburg: founded in 1723 by Peter the Great, Yekaterinburg is the capital of the Urals. Known as the Great Divide, the Ural Mountains create the natural border between Europe and Asia so that the cultural and architectural influences of European and Asian civilisations come together in this fascinating and cosmopolitan landscape. We will also visit Novosibirsk – the city is located in the heart of Russia and is situated on both banks of the river Ob – and the city tour will take us to Lenin Square where the imposing Opera House is located.

- **Day 7:** Few natural sights can surpass the beauty and grandeur of Lake Baikal, and this leg of our adventure is a major highlight on our Trans-Siberian journey. Lake Baikal is the deepest lake in the world and holds 20 per cent of the world's fresh water. Weather permitting, we will stop at an extremely picturesque location by the lake for photo opportunities and, for the brave-hearted, there is time for a refreshing swim in the crystal clear and ice-cold waters of Baikal.

- **Day 10:** Our Trans-Siberian adventure takes us into Mongolia and includes a visit to its capital, Ulaanbaatar. Mongolia, once the very centre of an enormous empire led by Genghis Khan, is a country laden with beautiful landscapes, nomadic people and is rich in culture and history.

- **Day 12:** Our train tracks the Chinese border along the Shilka and Amur rivers. This takes us across a dramatic, remote area of Siberia, where the ground is permanently frozen beneath the surface.

- **Day 14:** After covering a staggering 11,000km along this iconic railway, the *Golden Eagle* will glide into its final station of our adventure, Vladivostok. The city is an important, strategic military port located on the western shores of the Sea of Japan and is home to the Russian navy's Pacific Fleet. Vladivostok (literally translated as 'Ruler of the East') offers visitors an interesting opportunity to explore its principal military attractions, including a visit to a well-preserved World War II submarine.

Carefully read through the passage on the previous page and circle the correct answers below.

1 What is the name of the train on the Trans-Siberian Express route?

A. The *Orient Express*

B. The *Golden Eagle*

C. The *Asian Flyer*

D. The *Moscow Steamer*

---

2 How many time zones are there in the world?

A. Eight

B. 12

C. 24

D. 36

---

3 What will be the highlight of the Moscow part of the trip?

A. A trip to the Opera House

B. A visit to Lake Baikal

C. A meeting with Genghis Khan

D. A visit to the Kremlin and Red Square

---

4 What were the rulers of Russia known as historically?

A. Knights

B. Kings

C. Tsars

D. Monarchs

/4

5 What are the Ural Mountains also known as?

A. The Great Divide

B. The Steppes

C. The Himalayas

D. The Alps

---

6 Where is the Opera House located in Novosibirsk?

A. Next to Red Square

B. On the banks of Lake Baikal

C. Next to the Kremlin

D. Lenin Square

---

7 Which empire did Genghis Khan once preside over?

A. The Mongolian Empire

B. The British Empire

C. The Russian Empire

D. The Japanese Empire

---

8 Where is Vladivostok?

A. In Outer Mongolia

B. On the western shores of the Sea of Japan

C. It is a port on the shores of the South China Sea.

D. In mainland Nepal

/4

Comprehension 14

The Tour de France

The Tour de France is the most prestigious men's cycling race in the world, covering approximately 3500km. It is renowned for being the most challenging competition in the sport, attracting cyclists from across the globe. The race was founded in 1903 by a French cyclist and journalist called Henri Desgrange. Three years prior, Desgrange's newspaper, *L'Auto*, was first issued and printed on yellow
5   paper, rather than the green paper used by a rival racing newspaper called *Le Vélo*. This is where the inspiration for the signature yellow jersey came from. Each day, or 'stage' as they're called in the race, the yellow jersey is awarded to the cyclist who achieved the fastest time. The cyclist who manages to race the most stages in the shortest amount of time wins overall.

There are four types of jersey used to reward the best riders. While the yellow jersey is awarded to the
10   winner from the day before, the green jersey is worn by the fastest sprinter. Erik Zabel is the current record-holder after winning the final green jersey in 1996, 2001 and every year in between. The 'King of the Mountains' polka dot jersey is given to the cyclist who has received the most points in the climbing stages, with more points awarded to those who are the first to finish particularly difficult climbs. A climb's difficulty is determined by considering both its length and average steepness. Finally,
15   the white jersey is won by the fastest cyclist under the age of 25.

Approximately 22 professional teams compete annually, with each team made up of eight cyclists. There are various different types of racing; organisers plan to include all of them, or at least an appropriate balance, so that the race tests various strengths. Cyclists must be able to excel at flat, rolling stages, as well as routes through mountainous regions, while maintaining their stamina to reach the
20   final stage. This is incredibly challenging as cyclists tend to either excel at climbing hills and mountains or in time trials; it is the athlete's flexibility of strengths that separates them from other contestants. This explains why the Tour de France is known as a supreme test of athletic endurance.

Teamwork is integral to a cyclist's success in the competition. This is because the team uses a range of tactics to help the leader. Tactics include riding ahead of the leader to protect him from the wind,
25   assisting if he has a flat tyre, setting the pace when on a particularly challenging part of the race and making calculated attacks on rival teams, forcing them to slow down. Although it is the leader who appears in a yellow jersey, labelled 'winner' by major news outlets globally, the winner's prize is still shared among the team. This happens as there would be no success for the leader without the clever and strategic team that worked with him.

30   The race has been the subject of controversy and debate, as the event has always been, and still is, an all-male race. Smaller races, designated to women, have been established, but there is a massive disparity in distance, difficulty and prize money. In 2020, however, Christian Prudhomme, the general director of the competition, told *Le Telegramme* that they were in the process of creating a women's stage race.

Reportedly, in the Tour de France's most recent event, the numbers of people tuning in to watch the
35   final stage of the race play out on their television screens exceeded seven million. This is unsurprising considering how successfully it has run for over a century. Since its creation, the race has run every year except for two short breaks during the World Wars.

Carefully read through the passage on the previous page and circle the correct answers below.

1 'The cyclist who manages to race the most stages…' (lines 7 and 8)

What does the word 'stages' mean?

A. Mountains in the race

B. Segments of the race

C. Days of the race

D. Time trials in the race

2 Which of the following is not a tactic utilised by the teams to help their leader?

A. Launching strategic attacks on rival teams to slow them down

B. Setting a slow pace when the leader is tired and needs a rest

C. Assisting if his bicycle's tyre becomes too deflated

D. Speeding up to ride ahead and offer the leader some shielding from winds

3 In which year was *L'Auto* first published?

A. 1903

B. 1901

C. 1906

D. 1900

4 What must be considered in order to determine a climb's difficulty level?

A. The climb's distance and the mean degree of its gradient

B. The length of the climb and the wind speeds

C. The altitude of the climb and the length of the climb

D. The road surface and the wind speeds

/4

5 For how many consecutive years did Erik Zabel win the green jersey?

A. Two years

B. Four years

C. Three years

D. Six years

---

6 Why is the competition sometimes a point of contention?

A. Some believe it is not challenging enough for the athletes.

B. It seems unfair that only the leader gets to be labelled as the winner.

C. Only men can compete in the race and there is currently no equivalent for women.

D. It is too dangerous for the athletes.

---

7 According to the text, what is it that sets a particularly strong contestant apart from the crowd?

A. The flexibility of the athlete's body

B. The athlete's stamina

C. The athlete's ability to exploit his wide range of strengths

D. The strategic team that assists and protects the athlete

---

8 'Teamwork is integral to a cyclist's success...' (line 23)

What does 'integral' mean?

A. Handy

B. Essential

C. Irrelevant

D. Equal

/4

Comprehension 15

Banksy

In the early 1990s, an anonymous street artist began spray-painting trains and walls across Bristol, a city well known for its vibrant street art and graffiti. The pieces all had an incredibly unique style and, as a result, people soon concluded that they were most likely all pieces of work created by the same artist.

During the decade that followed, the artist's work was being discovered beyond the confines of Bristol.
5   The artist became known as Banksy, and would soon be leaving his artistic mark all over the world, with pieces of art now spread globally across countries such as Australia, Spain, England, the United States, Canada, Israel and more.

Early on, Banksy's art was influenced by the likes of Blek le Rat, a French graffiti artist. As a result, he was inspired to send political messages through his work and use a stencil technique, which he still uses a lot
10 today. There was, however, another important advantage to using stencils, as it proved to be a far more time-efficient method. This meant he could maintain his anonymity with greater ease. The rats that appear as a recurring theme in his work are also inspired by Blek le Rat and, at a London exhibition, he even released 200 of them in the gallery.

Banksy spent a month in New York during the autumn of 2013 and unveiled a new piece of work every
15 day. Halfway through his stay, he stood in Central Park pretending to be an ordinary street seller where he only managed to sell eight pieces for $60 each. The next day he authenticated the canvases and the work could be sold on for an overwhelmingly large profit.

Banksy's artwork is a very contentious topic. While some consider it revolutionary and an outlet for crucial political statements, others consider it to be vandalism, and in some areas his graffiti has even been
20 painted over soon after it appears. Others question why Banksy's work is seen as a spectacle which should be protected and treasured while regular graffiti artists are prosecuted and sometimes even put in prison, as their artwork is labelled as criminal damage. Finally, some argue that Banksy's focus on his own anonymity ultimately acts as a restriction; it stops him from making any real contributions to change.

In 2014, a piece called *Spy Booth* was painted onto the side of a listed building in Cheltenham. It framed
25 a phonebooth and depicted men in 1950s-style clothes spying by listening in on, and recording, the conversations taking place inside the phonebooth. A year later, a businessman called Hekmat Kaveh applied for the work, satellite dish and phonebooth to be included in the property's Grade II* listed status. Only two years after it first appeared, the piece disappeared, leaving a pile of rubble and plaster. It is unknown whether it was destroyed or if it was removed from the building and kept intact.

30 As Banksy's artwork often appears on walls or buildings in public places, there is much debate as to who technically owns it. This is particularly controversial when the pieces up for debate are valuable ones, and his work often sells for a lot of money. A piece called *Keep It Simple* sold for over £1m. Banksy's art is estimated to be worth more than £15m annually. Sometimes the art is left where it is to be enjoyed by the public, and these are now considered to be tourist attractions. When the art is sold, however, Banksy
35 does not keep the money from his sales. Instead, he adopts a philanthropic position and requests that it be donated towards charities.

Banksy is considered to be one of the world's most famous modern-day artists, which is why his ability to keep his identity hidden is so remarkable.

Carefully read through the passage on the previous page and circle the correct answers below.

1 In which decade was Banksy's art first discovered?

A. The last decade of the 19th century

B. The first decade of the 20th century

C. The last decade of the 20th century

D. The first decade of the 19th century

2 In the application for *Spy Booth* to be included in the Cheltenham house's Grade II* listed status, what did this application not protect?

A. The plaster

B. The phonebooth

C. The satellite dish

D. The artwork

3 Why do some people deem Banksy to be a philanthropist?

A. He leaves his art where it can be enjoyed by the public.

B. When he sells his art, he donates the money to charities.

C. He doesn't sell his artworks; he gives them away.

D. He creates art that attracts tourists.

4 What is debatable about his work being on walls and the sides of buildings in public?

A. The artwork's value

B. The artwork's legitimacy

C. The artwork's ownership

D. The artwork's effect

/4

5 Which one of the following statements is true?

A. Banksy is a political pioneer.

B. People believe that Banksy cannot bring about real change if he continues to live and work incognito.

C. Blek le Rat once released 200 rats in an art gallery.

D. The stencil technique made Banksy's work neater.

---

6 In which city did Banksy pretend to be an ordinary street seller?

A. New York

B. Bristol

C. London

D. Israel

---

7 In which year did *Spy Booth* mysteriously disappear?

A. 2014

B. 2015

C. 2016

D. 2017

---

8 What is the approximate annual value of Banksy's artwork?

A. Less than £15m

B. More than £1m

C. Approximately £1m

D. Over £15m

/4

Comprehension 16

The War of the Worlds

From *The War of the Worlds*, Chapter 4, 'The Cylinder Opens', by HG Wells

This novel is set in England in the late 19th century. In this excerpt, a cylindrical Thing from outer space has landed, creating an enormous pit in which it is now embedded. A crowd of onlookers has gathered, and both scientists (including the astronomer, Stent) and townspeople are mystified.

The end of the cylinder was being screwed out from within. Nearly two feet of shining screw projected. Somebody blundered against me, and I narrowly missed being pitched onto the top of the screw. I turned, and as I did so, the screw must have come out, for the lid of the cylinder fell upon the gravel with a ringing concussion. I stuck my elbow into the person behind me, and turned my head towards the
5   Thing again. For a moment that circular cavity seemed perfectly black. I had the sunset in my eyes.

I think everyone expected to see a man emerge – possibly something a little unlike us terrestrial men, but in all essentials a man. I know I did. But, looking, I presently saw something stirring within the shadow: greyish billowy movements, one above another, and then two luminous disks – like eyes. Then, something resembling a little grey snake, about the thickness of a walking stick, coiled up out of the
10   writhing middle, and wriggled in the air towards me – and then another.

A sudden chill came over me. There was a loud shriek from a woman behind. I half turned, keeping my eyes fixed upon the cylinder still, from which other tentacles were now projecting, and began pushing my way back from the edge of the pit. I saw astonishment giving place to horror on the faces of the people about me. I heard inarticulate exclamations on all sides. There was a general movement backwards. I saw
15   the young shop assistant, who had been bumped into the pit by the jostling crowd; he was struggling still on the edge of the pit. I found myself alone, and saw the people on the other side of the pit running off, Stent among them. I looked again at the cylinder, and ungovernable terror gripped me. I stood petrified and staring.

A big greyish rounded bulk, the size, perhaps, of a bear, was rising slowly and painfully out of the
20   cylinder. As it bulged up and caught the light, it glistened like wet leather.

Two large dark-coloured eyes were regarding me steadfastly. The mass that framed them, the head of the thing, was rounded, and had, one might say, a face. There was a mouth under the eyes, the lipless brim of which quivered and panted, and dropped saliva. The whole creature heaved and pulsated convulsively. A lank tentacular appendage gripped the edge of the cylinder, another swayed in the air.

25   Those who have never seen a living Martian can scarcely imagine the strange horror of its appearance. The peculiar V-shaped mouth with its pointed upper lip, the absence of brow ridges, the absence of a chin beneath the wedgelike lower lip, the incessant quivering of the mouth, the Gorgon groups of tentacles, the tumultuous breathing of the lungs in a strange atmosphere, the evident heaviness and painfulness of movement due to the greater gravitational energy of Earth – above all, the extraordinary intensity of
30   the immense eyes – were at once vital, intense, inhuman, crippled and monstrous. There was something fungoid in the oily brown skin, something in the clumsy deliberation of the tedious movements unspeakably nasty. Even at this first encounter, this first glimpse, I was overcome with disgust and dread.

Suddenly, the monster vanished. It had toppled over the brim of the cylinder and fallen into the pit, with a thud like the fall of a great mass of leather. I heard it give a peculiar thick cry, and forthwith another of these creatures appeared darkly in the deep shadow of the aperture.

I turned and, running madly, made for the first group of trees, perhaps a hundred yards away; but I ran slantingly and stumbling, for I could not avert my face from these things.

There, among some young pine trees and furze bushes, I stopped, panting, and waited for further developments. The common around the sand pits was dotted with people, standing like myself in a half-fascinated terror, staring at these creatures, or rather at the heaped gravel at the edge of the pit in which they lay. And then, with a renewed horror, I saw a round, black object bobbing up and down on the edge of the pit. It was the head of the shopman who had fallen in, but showing as a little black object against the hot western sun. Now he got his shoulder and knee up, and again he seemed to slip back until only his head was visible. Suddenly he vanished, and I could have fancied a faint shriek had reached me. I had a momentary impulse to go back and help him that my fears overruled.

Carefully read through the passage on the previous page and above and circle the correct answers below.

1 When does the story in this novel take place?

A. Between the years 1951 and 1999

B. Between the years 1801 and 1849

C. Between the years 1901 and 1949

D. Between the years 1851 and 1899

---

2 How many creatures did the author observe emerging from the cylinder?

A. It is not clear from the text.

B. Two

C. Four

D. Three

---

3 Why didn't the author help rescue the young shop assistant?

A. Because he noticed that another man had already rushed to his aid.

B. Because he instinctively knew that it was too late to save the man.

C. Because he was too terrified to return to the edge of the crater.

D. Because he was the man's enemy so he was reluctant to help.

/3

4 What was significant about the Martian's chin?

A. It was forked and sharp.

C. It was a slimy leather-like protuberance.

B. It was non-existent.

D. It had tentacles hanging from it.

---

5 Which one of the following statements is true?

A. The author anticipated that a human-like figure would surface from the Thing.

B. The crowd were initially fascinated and slowly edged forward towards the Thing.

C. The screw that sealed the Thing was more than three metres in length.

D. The shopman managed to raise his entire body from the crater before falling back in.

---

6 Who let out a high-pitched scream within earshot of the author?

A. The shop assistant

B. A man standing to his left

C. A lady from farther back in the crowd

D. The Martian

---

7 Which one of the following statements is true?

A. The author fled purposely for the trees after one of the monsters vanished.

B. Initially, the Martian appeared to have three eyes.

C. The Martian had a very slender frame.

D. The Martian was dribbling when it first emerged from the Thing.

---

8 Which one of the following words is a synonym for 'inarticulate'? (line 14)

A. Incoherent

C. Inconsistent

B. Inaudible

D. Intense

/5

Answers

Extended answers with useful explanations are available online at
www.scholastic.co.uk/pass-your-11-plus/extras or via the QR code opposite.

1. The *Mona Lisa*
pp.5–8

1	B
2	A
3	D
4	C
5	B
6	A
7	A
8	C
9	D
10	C

2. Alfred Nobel
pp.9–12

1	C
2	B
3	A
4	A
5	B
6	D
7	D
8	C
9	B
10	C

3. Jane Austen
pp.13–16

1	D
2	C
3	B
4	D
5	A
6	B
7	D
8	A
9	B
10	C

4. San Francisco
pp.17–20

1	A
2	D
3	C
4	B
5	D
6	C
7	A
8	B
9	D
10	C

5. London
pp.21–24

1	D
2	B
3	C
4	A
5	D
6	B
7	A
8	C
9	D
10	D

6. Obituary: Amelia Earhart
pp.25–28

1	A
2	D
3	C
4	B
5	B
6	C
7	A
8	D
9	A
10	C

7. Houses for Sale
pp.29–32

1	B
2	D
3	B
4	A
5	C
6	B
7	D
8	C
9	A
10	D

8. Victorian Child Labour
pp.33–36

1	C
2	A
3	D
4	B
5	D
6	B
7	C
8	A
9	C
10	D

Answers

9. The Hermitage Museum
pp.37–39

1	B
2	C
3	D
4	B
5	A
6	C
7	C
8	A

10. The Diaries of Florence Nightingale
pp.40–43

1	C
2	D
3	C
4	A
5	B
6	C
7	D
8	A

11. Amazing Animals of Africa
pp.44–46

1	C
2	B
3	A
4	C
5	A
6	D
7	C
8	B

12. Thomas Cook
pp.47–49

1	C
2	A
3	D
4	A
5	B
6	C
7	D
8	D

13. The Longest Train Journey in the World
pp.50–52

1	B
2	C
3	D
4	C
5	A
6	D
7	A
8	B

14. Tour de France
pp.53–55

1	C
2	B
3	D
4	A
5	D
6	C
7	C
8	B

15. Banksy
pp.56–58

1	C
2	A
3	B
4	C
5	B
6	A
7	C
8	D

16. *The War of the Worlds*
pp.59–61

1	D
2	A
3	C
4	B
5	A
6	C
7	D
8	A

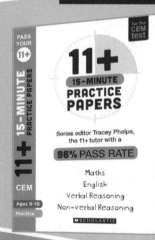 
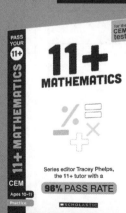